INTRO TO PHYSICS Need to Know

SilverTip

Motion

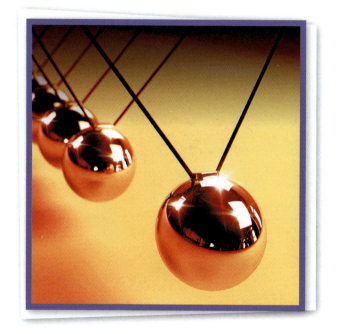

by Karen Latchana Kenney

Consultant: Kathy Renfrew
Science Educator and Science Learner

BEARPORT
PUBLISHING

Minneapolis, Minnesota

Credits

Cover and title page, © dottedhippo/iStock; 5, © VIAVAL TOURS/Shutterstock; 7, © wizdata/Shutterstock; 9, © NassornSnitwong/Shutterstock; 10–11, © Kiwis/iStock; 13, © xavierarnau/Shutterstock; 15TL, © T.W. van Urk/Shutterstock; 15TC, © Kconstantine/Shutterstock; 15TR, © anutr tosirikul/Shutterstock; 15BL, © Jakov Simovic/Shutterstock; 15BC, © Dmitriy Prayzel/Shutterstock; 15BR, © borchee/iStock; 17T, © musicman/Shutterstock; 17C, © Patty Chan/Shutterstock; 17B, © justoomm/Shutterstock; 19, © Morphart Creation/Shutterstock; 21, © yamasan0708/Shutterstock; 23T, © Michael Potter11/Shutterstock; 23B, © Visual Intermezzo/Shutterstock; 24, © Jose Antonio Perez/Shutterstock; 25, © icsnaps/Shutterstock; 27, © Gorodenkoff/Shutterstock; and 28, © VectorMine/Shutterstock.

Bearport Publishing Company Product Development Team

President: Jen Jenson; Director of Product Development: Spencer Brinker; Senior Editor: Allison Juda; Editor: Charly Haley; Associate Editor: Naomi Reich; Senior Designer: Colin O'Dea; Associate Designer: Elena Klinkner; Product Development Assistant: Anita Stasson

Library of Congress Cataloging-in-Publication Data is available at www.loc.gov or upon request from the publisher.

ISBN: 979-8-88509-225-8 (hardcover)
ISBN: 979-8-88509-232-6 (paperback)
ISBN: 979-8-88509-239-5 (ebook)

Copyright © 2023 Bearport Publishing Company. All rights reserved. No part of this publication may be reproduced in whole or in part, stored in any retrieval system, or transmitted in any form or by any means, electronic, mechanical, photocopying, recording, or otherwise, without written permission from the publisher.

For more information, write to Bearport Publishing, 5357 Penn Avenue South, Minneapolis, MN 55419. Printed in the United States of America.

Contents

Using Hills for Thrills 4
Going the Distance 6
Use the Force 10
Full Contact. 12
From Near and Far 16
Forced to Follow Rules. 18
Movement Math. 22
All Is Equal 24
Moving Forward 26

Newton's Laws of Motion 28
SilverTips for Success 29
Glossary 30
Read More 31
Learn More Online 31
Index 32
About the Author 32

Using Hills for Thrills

The roller coaster cars slowly creak to the top of a huge hill. And that's where the fun begins. You make it over the hump and speed down the hill, hurtling onward along the track. This coaster uses physics for fun!

> Most roller coasters use hills to build up **energy** for the rest of the ride. The pull of **gravity** during the first drop is what gets it all going.

Going the Distance

We know roller coasters zoom along tracks. But how do we measure their motion? Speed tells us how fast something moves. This shows how long it takes for a coaster car to move along part of the tracks.

Roller coasters also have **velocity**. This combines speed and direction.

> If you are biking north and it takes an hour to go 10 miles (16 km), your speed is 10 miles per hour (16 kph). And your velocity is 10 miles per hour north.

The velocity of a moving object can change over a distance. This is called **acceleration**. When objects speed up or slow down, they accelerate. Objects also accelerate if they change direction as they move.

Some people use the term deceleration. But it is actually negative acceleration. When you hit the brakes, you slow down. Since this rate of change is getting smaller, it is a negative acceleration.

Use the Force

Now we know how to measure it. But what makes motion happen? Things need a **force** to get going.

At their most basic, forces are pushes or pulls. They give objects energy. Often, this energy makes things move.

When you ride a bike, force comes from your feet. They push the pedals, which makes the bicycle move forward. For cars, engines provide the force to move.

Full Contact

There are many different kinds of forces. Some work when two objects touch, such as when you kick a soccer ball. These are called contact forces. Objects can make contact in different ways. And they **react** to contact differently, too.

Many contact forces are easy to see. But sometimes these forces are a little trickier to spot. For example, air makes a kite fly high. Wind can cause motion even if we can't see the actual air.

The kick to a soccer ball is a kind of pushing contact force called an applied force. **Resistance** from the air and **friction** rubbing against the ground are contact forces, too. They slow the ball. A normal contact force keeps that soccer ball still when it comes to a rest.

Tension is a contact force that gets energy from pulling in opposite directions. A tug-of-war rope has tension. Springs also have contact forces. These forces pull or push as springs stretch and compress.

Contact Forces

| Applied force | Friction | Tension |

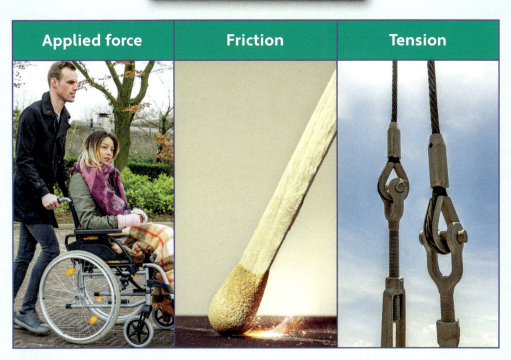

| Normal force | Spring force | Air resistance |

From Near and Far

Some forces push and pull on objects without direct contact. These are called distant forces.

Gravity pulls large objects together. Magnets push or pull other magnets without ever touching. And electricity has a force that works at a distance, too.

> Distant forces can work from far away. But there is a limit to how far. As things get farther from Earth, the planet's gravity does not pull as strongly.

Forced to Follow Rules

Movement can be caused by different kinds of forces. But it always follows some of the same rules. The first scientist to describe motion was Sir Isaac Newton. He wrote about his three laws of motion in the 1600s. These ideas about how motion works are still used today!

> Have you heard the story of the scientist who discovered gravity by watching an apple fall? That story is about Newton. But it was probably made up.

Sir Isaac Newton

Newton's first law says an object that is still will stay still. It also says that an object moving at a constant speed stays moving at that speed. This is called **inertia**. It only changes if another force acts on the object.

Have you been in a car that brakes quickly? The car stops suddenly, but your body may keep moving forward. Your body has inertia.

Movement Math

Newton's second law measures changes that happen to motion because of force. We know a force changes how fast an object moves and which direction it goes. Newton found that the force is equal to an object's **mass**, or the amount of stuff it has, times its acceleration.

> Why is it harder to lift an elephant than a ladybug? The large mammal has more mass than the small bug. So, you need to use more force to lift it up.

All Is Equal

The last of Newton's laws describes how forces affect two objects at the same time. When one object's force acts on another object, the second object reacts. It produces a force against the first object. That force is equal in strength and moves in the opposite direction.

Have you seen a spacecraft launch into the sky? The rocket's engine burns gases. It pushes those gases down with a force. The opposite reaction is that the spacecraft moves up.

Your hand pushes on a basketball and the ball pushes back.

Moving Forward

We have laws about how motion behaves and math to measure it. But we still don't know it all. Scientists continue to study motion. The more we know, the faster and more efficiently we can get where we need to go. Let's get moving!

> For a long time, researchers have studied the way our bodies move. With this information, they have been able to make a robotic skeleton to help people who cannot otherwise walk. What's next?

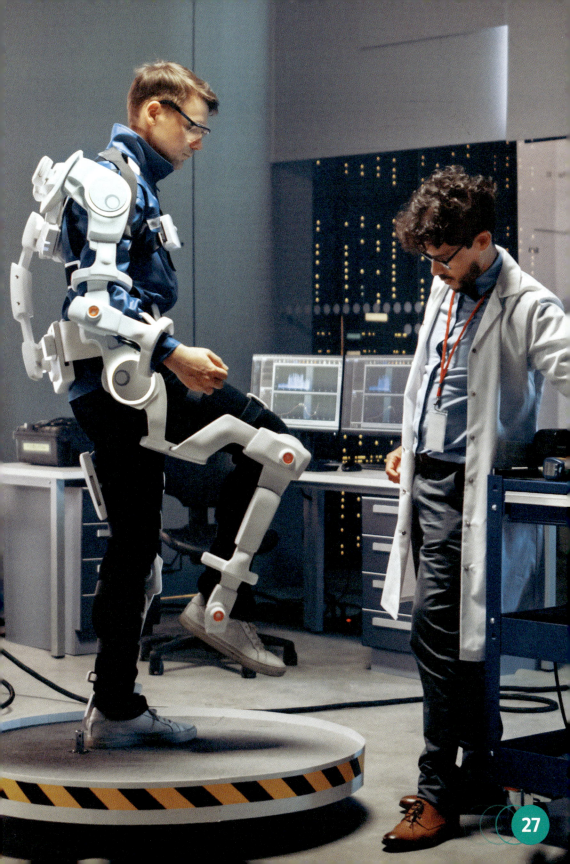

Newton's Laws of Motion

Law 1: The Law of Inertia

At rest, a grocery cart stays put. To get moving, it needs a force, such as a push.

Law 2: The Law of Mass and Acceleration

It takes more force to move objects with more mass. Objects with less mass accelerate more.

Law 3: The Law of Action and Reaction

Every action with a force makes an object react. This force is of the same amount going in the opposite direction.

SilverTips for SUCCESS

⭐ SilverTips for REVIEW

Review what you've learned. Use the text to help you.

Define key terms

contact forces   inertia
distant forces   velocity
forces

Check for understanding

Describe the difference between speed, velocity, and acceleration.

What is a contact force? Name three kinds of these forces.

How do distant forces differ from contact forces?

Think deeper

Think of a sport or activity with forces in motion. Describe how Newton's three laws of motion are at play during the activity.

⭐ SilverTips on TEST-TAKING

- **Make a study plan.** Ask your teacher what the test is going to cover. Then, set aside time to study a little bit every day.

- **Read all the questions carefully.** Be sure you know what is being asked.

- **Skip any questions** you don't know how to answer right away. Mark them and come back later if you have time.

Glossary

acceleration the amount of change in an object's speed and direction

energy power that can make something happen, such as make an object move

force a push or pull that causes movement

friction a force that slows down objects that are rubbing against each other

gravity the force that pulls objects toward large objects, such as Earth

inertia a property that keeps an object still or moving based on what it is already doing

mass a measure of the amount or quantity of something

react to do something in response

resistance force that slows objects down

velocity the measure of how far something travels over a set period of time and in a direction

Read More

Amstutz, Lisa. *Science in Motion (Project: STEAM).* North Mankato, MN: Rourke Educational Media, 2019.

Faust, Daniel R. *Motion: Examining Interactions (Spotlight on Physical Science).* New York: PowerKids Press, 2020.

Hustad, Douglas. *The Science of Amusement Parks (The Science of Fun).* Minneapolis: Abdo Publishing, 2022.

Learn More Online

1. Go to **www.factsurfer.com** or scan the QR code below.
2. Enter "**Physics Motion**" into the search box.
3. Click on the cover of this book to see a list of websites.

Index

acceleration 8, 22, 28

contact forces 12, 14–16

distant forces 16

energy 4, 10, 14

gravity 4, 16, 18

inertia 20, 28

laws of motion 18, 20, 22, 24, 26, 28

mass 22, 28

measure 6, 10, 22, 26

Newton, Isaac 18–20, 22, 24, 28

react 12, 24, 28

speed 4, 6, 8, 20

velocity 6, 8

About the Author

Karen Latchana Kenney is an author from Minnesota. She loves riding her bicycle and visiting the places it takes her.